Abortion ban in America

Indiana abortion law; what you should know

Table of contents

Chapter 1

ABORTION BANS: IN THE STATES

Abortion bans are a deceitful and unlawful effort to outlaw abortions as early as 13 weeks in pregnancy. These laws severely interfere with the doctor-patient relationship, outlawing abortions that physicians claim are safe and among the best to preserve women's health. Prior to Gonzales v. Carhart ("Carhart II"). courts – including the United States Supreme Court in Stenberg v. Carhart ("Carhart") – considered these bans, and repeatedly and consistently struck them down for two reasons:

The bans' broad language prohibits abortions as early as 13 weeks in pregnancy, and\sThe bans' lack of health exception impermissibly endangers women's health. However, in Carhart II, the Supreme Court upheld the federal Partial-Birth Abortion Ban Act of 2003 despite its lack of a health exception. The Court concluded that the Act was not unconstitutionally vague because it defined the overt act and intent necessary for criminal liability. The Court also held that a health exception was unnecessary because of medical uncertainty over whether "the barred procedure is ever necessary to preserve a woman's health" and because of the availability of other abortion procedures. The Court left open the option of an as-applied constitutional challenge. (The ACLU's more in-depth discussion of the Supreme Court's decision in Carhart II upholding the federal ban is available online at https://www.aclu.org/reproductive-freedom/case-summaries-us-supreme-court-uph olds-federal-ban-abortion-methods.) Since 1995, abortion bans have been enacted in more than half the states and challenged in courts throughout the country. To date:

Thirty-one states have enacted one or more bans. (1)\sBans have been challenged and struck down in twenty states. (2)\sIn eight states, bans were not challenged in court but are either unenforceable under Carhart II for vagueness or are limited to abortions performed after viability. (3)\sIn one state (OH), courts have supported a prohibition on the argument that it did not cover the most prevalent abortion procedures and had a health exemption, although a restricted one.

In two states in which restrictions were challenged (GA, MT), the parties agreed, and courts ruled, that the bans would be confined to post-viability abortions.

In the four states (MI, MO, UT, VA) in which restrictions were challenged following Carhart II, one court (in MI) invalidated the ban as unconstitutional. In the other three states (MO, UT, VA), restrictions have been maintained. Michigan, like numerous other states (4), has subsequently implemented a statute replicating the federal prohibition. Those laws are in force.

In the three states in which similar abortion prohibitions have come up as ballot measures (CO, ME, and WA), voters rejected them.

Below is an overview of the court judgments in instances challenging state prohibitions.

Alabama: Summit Medical Associates v. Siegelman, 130 F. Supp. 2d 1307 (M.D. Ala. 2001). (M.D. Ala. 2001).

Following the ruling in Carhart, a federal district judge deemed the Alabama restriction unlawful and permanently blocked its implementation. The court ruled that the Alabama act, like the Nebraska provision struck down in Carhart, was unconstitutional for lack of a health exemption and because it put an unreasonable burden on a woman's right to abortion. Specifically, the court ruled that the Alabama Act would ban D&E [dilation and evacuation] abortions, the "most routinely utilized procedure for pre-viability second-trimester abortions." The state did not appeal the court's verdict.

Alaska: Planned Parenthood of Alaska, Inc. v. State, No. 3AN-97-6019 CIV (Alaska Super. Ct. Mar. 13, 1998), appeal dropped, No. S-08610 (Alaska June 29, 2000). (Alaska June 29, 2000).

A state trial judge permanently halted Alaska's "partial-birth abortion" ban, concluding that it violates the state constitution. The court found the statute unconstitutional for vagueness, finding the phrase "partial-birth abortion" so "susceptible to multiple interpretations" that it may "apply not just to second-trimester abortions but to certain first-trimester abortions as well." Because the rule may so act as a prohibition on "abortion in general," the court found that it offended the state's constitutional right to privacy. Following the Carhart judgment, the Alaska Attorney General dropped the State's appeal to the Supreme Court of Alaska.

Arizona: Planned Parenthood of Southern Arizona, Inc. v. Woods, 982 F. Supp. 1369 (D. Ariz. 1997), appeal withdrawn, No. 97-17377 (9th Cir. Feb. 26, 1999). (9th Cir. Feb. 26, 1999).

A federal district judge permanently barred Arizona's "partial-birth abortion" law. The court decided the restriction was unconstitutionally vague because it was "susceptible to alternative interpretations" and so failed to provide doctors fair notice of what behavior it outlawed. The court further ruled that the prohibition imposed an "undue burden" on the right to obtain an abortion since, in restricting the safest, most usual techniques of abortion beyond the first trimester, the ban would shift women from safer to riskier procedures. The State did not appeal the district court's judgment.

Arkansas: Little Rock Family Planning Services P.A. v. Jegley, No. LR-C-97-581 (E.D. Ark. Nov. 13, 1998), upheld, 192 F.3d 794 (8th Cir. 1999). (8th Cir. 1999).

Affirming a federal trial court's permanent injunction of Arkansas's prohibition, the U.S. Court of Appeals for the Eighth Circuit concluded that the statute would impermissibly restrict "both the D&E procedure and the suction-curettage technique," the two most prevalent abortion procedures. The appeal court concluded that such a prohibition was unconstitutionally "overbroad and imposing an undue burden on the right of a woman to determine whether to have an abortion." The State did not challenge the Eighth Circuit's verdict.

Florida: A Choice for Women v. Butterworth, 54 F. Supp. 2d 1148 (S.D. Fla. 1998), appeal dropped, No. 99-4002 (11th Cir. Mar. 2, 1999); A Choice for Women v. Butterworth, No. 00-1820-CIV-LENARD/TURNOFF, 2000 WL 34403086 (S.D. Fla. July 11, 2000). (S.D. Fla. July 11, 2000).

A federal district judge permanently blocked Florida's first effort, in 1998, to impose a so-called "partial-birth abortion" law. The court rejected the claim that the statute addressed a particular, distinct operation. Rather, the court ruled, that the law's definition featured "broad and imprecise language" that might encompass almost all abortions conducted in the second trimester of pregnancy. Thus, the court concluded that the prohibition infringed "a woman's freedom to choose to have an abortion before the viability of the fetus." The court also declared the restriction unlawful on the premise that it "contains no health exemption and only a qualified life exception."

Despite the court's unequivocal finding that such a ban was illegal, Florida implemented a second, differently-worded ban on May 25, 2000. Following the ruling in Carhart, a federal court deemed the second restriction illegal and imposed an injunction permanently prohibiting its implementation. The court concluded that the act's "sweeping prohibitions[s] … including D&E and D&X [dilation and extraction], creates an excessive burden and a significant impediment on a woman's right" to choose a pre-viability abortion. Moreover, the court decided that the restriction was unconstitutional since it lacked a health exemption. The State did not challenge the court's ruling.

Georgia: Midtown Hospital v. Miller, 36 F. Supp. 2d 1360 (N.D. GA. 1998). (N.D. GA. 1998).

A federal district judge ordered a preliminary injunction confining enforcement of Georgia's prohibition on post-viability abortions. The parties eventually resolved the matter by agreeing that the statute would apply only to a narrowly specified method when utilized after fetal viability. The court issued an order — called a consent decree — that made the deal enforceable.

Idaho: Weyhrich v. Lance, No. CV98-0117-S-BLW, 1999 WL 33884457 (D. Idaho Oct. 12, 1999) (D. Idaho Oct. 12, 1999)

A federal district judge ordered a permanent injunction blocking the implementation of Idaho's "partial-birth abortion" law. Finding the Language of the prohibition would possibly embrace "suction curettage, D&E, and induction procedures," the court concluded the restriction unconstitutionally put an excessive burden on the right to reproductive choice. The court also ruled that the statute was unconstitutional because 1) its words were "so hopelessly ambiguous that doctors simply cannot know what activity it bans," 2) the prohibition lacked an exemption to safeguard women's health, and 3) it lacked a sufficient exception to protect their lives.

Illinois: Hope Clinic v. Ryan, 995 F. Supp. 847 (N.D. Ill. 1998), reversed, 195 F.3d 857 (7th Cir. 1999) (en banc), stay refused, 197 F.3d 876 (7th Cir. 1999), vacated and remanded, 530 U.S. 1271 (2000), 249 F.3d 603 (7th Cir. 2001). (7th Cir. 2001).

A federal district judge ordered a permanent injunction barring the implementation of Illinois's "partial-birth abortion" prohibition. Finding that the statute potentially outlawed the most popular and safest abortion techniques performed throughout pregnancy, the trial court concluded the law was unconstitutional for infringing the right to reproductive choice. The court also concluded the provision was unconstitutionally vague because the "statute, packed with indeterminate phrases, fails to describe with any certainty the activity that is proscribed."

The State appealed to the U.S. Court of Appeals for the Seventh Circuit. Initially, the court sustained the restriction on the condition that lower courts define the rule narrowly and limit its scope. Following the ruling in Carhart, however, the Seventh Circuit ruled the Illinois restriction was unconstitutional and sustained the lower court's permanent injunction prohibiting enforcement. In the same ruling, the court also ruled the Wisconsin prohibition unlawful and permanently enjoined.

Iowa: Planned Parenthood of Greater Iowa, Inc. v. Miller, 30 F. Supp. 2d 1157 (S.D. Iowa 1998), affirmed, 195 F.3d 386 (8th Cir. 1999), cert. denied, 120 S. Ct. 2801 (2000). (2000).

The U.S. Court of Appeals for the Eighth Circuit confirmed a federal trial court's finding that permanently blocked Iowa's "partial-birth abortion" prohibition. The Eighth Circuit found that the restriction forbids "the D&E operation, and, in certain situations, the suction-curettage treatment as well." Finding that these "are two of the most widely utilized abortion procedures," the court found that the restriction "places an unreasonable burden on women seeking abortions." The U.S. Supreme Court refused to consider the case.

Kentucky: Eubanks v. Stengel, 28 F. Supp. 2d 1024 (W.D. Ky. 1998), affirmed, 224 F.3d 576 (6th Cir. 2000). (6th Cir. 2000).

Following the judgment in Carhart, the U.S. Court of Appeals for the Sixth Circuit confirmed the lower court's order that permanently banned Kentucky's "partial-birth abortion" law. In its short judgment, the court decided that "[Carhart] is controlling in this instance, and that the district court was right when it ruled that the Kentucky Act is unconstitutional." Emphasizing that the broad scope of the ban created a "quagmire of constitutional infirmity," the lower court had held that by "banning a set of actions and results that embrace common and otherwise legal abortion procedures," the law placed "an undue burden upon a large fraction of those women whom the Act will affect."

Louisiana: Causeway Medical Suite v. Foster, 43 F. Supp. 2d 604 (E.D. La. 1999), affirmed, 221 F.3d 811 (5th Cir. 2000). (5th Cir. 2000).

Following the judgment in Carhart, the U.S. Court of Appeals for the Fifth Circuit confirmed the lower court's order that permanently banned Louisiana's "partial-birth abortion" law. The lower court ruled that the prohibition caused an undue burden since it lacked a health exemption and an adequate life exception while noting that the restriction served no purpose other than to make abortions more difficult.

Michigan: Evans v. Kelley, 977 F. Supp. 1283 (E.D. Mich. 1997); WomanCare of Southfield, P.C. v. Granholm, 143 F. Supp. 2d 849 (E.D. Mich. 2001); Northland Family Planning Clinic, Inc. v. Cox, 394 F. Supp. 2d 978 (E.D. Mich. 2005), affirmed, 487 F.3d 323 (6th Cir. 2007), cert. denied, 552 U.S. 1096 (2008). (2008).

In 1997, a federal district judge in Detroit deemed Michigan's prohibition unlawful and permanently blocked its implementation. The court ruled the statute was unconstitutionally vague because – given confusing and non-medical terms – doctors "simply cannot determine with any degree of confidence" what practices it

restricts. The court further invalidated the statute as an "undue burden" on the right
of a woman to choose to terminate her pregnancy, since "it would operate to
abolish one of the safest post-first trimester abortion procedures," D&E, the
method utilized in the great majority of post-first trimester abortions.

Notwithstanding this judgment, in 1999, Michigan approved a parallel but
differently worded bill. Following the ruling in Carhart, the district court declared
the second Michigan prohibition unconstitutional of the lack of "sufficient
exemption to preserve the mental and/or physical health of the pregnant woman."
The court imposed a permanent injunction barring the execution of the restriction.
The State did not appeal.

Undeterred, in 2004, the Michigan House approved yet a third restriction, this time
termed the "Legal Birth Definition Act." This legislation, wider than Michigan's
previous two abortion bans, barred even first-trimester abortions. In September
2005, a federal district court granted the plaintiff's petition for summary judgment
and permanently enjoined the statute. The court found that under Carhart, the
legislation was unconstitutional because it offered only a "meaningless" health
exemption and barred a spectrum of safe abortion techniques.

 The court quashed the prohibition on the additional grounds that its life exemption
did not appropriately safeguard women's lives and that it was ambiguous. After
Carhart II, the Sixth Circuit affirmed the district court's invalidation of the statute,
and held that the district court's determination that the "statue created an
unconstitutional undue burden on a woman's right to terminate her pregnancy …
has in no way been undermined by the interim decision in [Carhart II]." The Sixth
Circuit considered it unnecessary to analyze the implications of Carhart II for the
life and health exceptions of the laws because of its judgment that the general ban
itself was unconstitutional.

Missouri: Reproductive Health Services of Planned Parenthood v. Nixon, No.
99-04231-CV-C-SOW-ECF (W.D. Mo. Sept. 22, 1999), stay granted, No.
00-1310WMKC (8th Cir. Mar 23, 2000); State v. Reproductive Health Services of
Planned Parenthood, No. 22004-00008 (Mo. Cir. Ct. Dec. 5, 2000), modified, 97
S.W.3d 54 (Mo. Ct. App. 2002), cert. denied, SC 85051 (Mo. Mar. 4, 2003),

Reproductive Health Services of Planned Parenthood v. Nixon, 325 F. Supp. 2d 991 (W.D. Mo. 2004), affirmed, 429 F.3d 803 (8th Cir. 2005), cert granted, judgment vacated, 550 U.S. 901 (2007), injunction vacated, No. 04-2908 (8th Cir. 2007), dismissed by No. 99-04321-CV-C-SOW (W.D. Mo. 2007). (W.D. Mo. 2007).

In 1999, a federal trial court imposed a temporary restraining order prohibiting the implementation of Missouri's prohibition. Subsequently, Missouri proceeded to the state court to overcome the constitutional inadequacies of the statute by having the prohibition narrowly defined. The federal court proceedings were delayed awaiting the outcome of the state court action. The lower state court held that although a health exception was not explicitly in the text of the law, such an exception could be read into the statute. This determination was reversed by a state appeals court and the temporary restraining order remained in effect. The Missouri Supreme Court denied further review in the state case and the U.S. proceedings. In 2004, a federal trial court granted the plaintiff's petition for summary judgment, saying that the restriction is unconstitutional for lack of a health exemption. IN 2005 the U.S. Court of Appeals for the Eighth Circuit confirmed that ruling.

After upholding the federal abortion restriction in Carhart II, the Supreme Court vacated the Eighth Circuit ruling and returned the injunction for review in light of Carhart II. On remand, the Eighth Circuit vacated the injunction, and the prohibition remains in force.

Montana: Intermountain Planned Parenthood v. State, No. BDV 97-477 (Mont. Dist. Ct. June 29, 2998); Intermountain Planned Parenthood v. State, No. ADV 9900561 (Mont. Dist. Ct. March 21, 2000). (Mont. Dist. Ct. March 21, 2000).

A state district judge permanently enjoined Montana's "partial-birth abortion" prohibition. The court found that the statute "has the effect of banning D&E abortion procedures," which are used in 88 percent of second-trimester abortions in the state, and would thus "reduce a woman's access to abortion services, and increase the amount of risk and pain to the woman."

Following this ruling, the state passed an amended version of the ban. The state district court issued a temporary restraining order against the enforcement of the amended law. Later, based on an agreement between the parties, the court issued a permanent injunction limiting the amended ban to apply only to a narrowly defined procedure when used after fetal viability.

Nebraska: Stenberg v. Carhart, 530 U.S. 914 (2000), affirming, 192 F.3d 1142 (8th Cir. 1999), affirming, 11 F. Supp. 2d 1099 (D. Neb. 1998). (D. Neb. 1998).

In 2000, confirming a permanent injunction that the 8th Circuit had already maintained, the United States Supreme Court ruled Nebraska's "partial-birth abortion" prohibition unconstitutional on two distinct grounds, any of which alone would have been sufficient to strike down the law: 1) the ban's refusal to include a health exemption jeopardized women's health, and 2) the ban's wording embraced the most prevalent form of second-trimester abortion, so putting an excessive burden on women seeking abortions.

For a more in-depth explanation of the Supreme Court's ruling, read Stenberg v. Carhart: A Legal Analysis accessible online at https://www.aclu.org/reproductiverights/abortionbans/12513res20000701.html

New Jersey: Planned Parenthood of Central New Jersey v. Verniero, 41 F. Supp. 2d 478 (D.N.J. 1998), affirmed sub-nom. Planned Parenthood of Central New Jersey v. Farmer, 220 F.3d 127 (3rd Cir. 2000). (3rd Cir. 2000).

Following the judgment in Carhart, the U.S. Court of Appeals for the Third Circuit confirmed the lower court's order that permanently banned New Jersey's "partial-birth abortion" law. The Third Circuit concluded that the prohibition was legally invalid because it was "so vague as to embrace practically all kinds of abortion." Moreover, it ruled that the restriction presented an undue hardship since it would deter doctors from administering the "safest, most prevalent and easily accessible traditional pre- and post-viability abortion procedures" including, "suction and curettage, D&E and induction abortions."

Ohio: Women's Medical Professional Corp. v Voinovich, 911 F. Supp. 1051 (S.D. Ohio 1995), affirmed, 130 F.3d 187 (6th Cir. 1997), cert. denied, 523 U.S. 1036 (1998); Women's Medical Professional Corp. v. Taft, 162 F. Supp. 2d 929 (S.D. Ohio 2001), reversed, 353 F3d 436 (6th Cir. 2003), petition for rehearing en banc denied, No. 01-4124, 2004 U.S. App. LEXIS 7791 (6th Cir. Apr. 1, 2004). (6th Cir. Apr. 1, 2004).

In 1997, the U.S. Court of Appeals for the Sixth Circuit confirmed the district court judgment permanently enjoining an Ohio legislation that barred "dilation and extraction." In confirming the verdict, the Sixth Circuit ruled that the legislation constituted an unreasonable burden by, in effect, barring pre-viability D&E operations and "because it does not enable post-viability abortions if necessary" to maintain the woman's mental health. The U.S. Supreme Court refused to consider the case.

Following the decision in Carhart, Ohio passed a second abortion ban. A federal district court initially issued a permanent injunction blocking its enforcement. In 2003, however, a Sixth Circuit panel maintained the prohibition, ruling the rule's limited health exemption adequate since it allowed doctors to conduct illegal abortions when required to safeguard women from serious health risks, even when such abortions would be safer than alternative techniques. The court also relied largely on the fact that the statute excluded D&E from its scope. The plaintiffs urge the entire Sixth Circuit (as distinguished from a three-judge panel) to rehear the matter. However, the Sixth Circuit denied this request. The plaintiffs did not seed further review by the U.S. Supreme Court.

Rhode Island: Rhode Island Medical Society v. Whitehouse, 66 F. Supp. 2d 288 (D.R.I. 1999), affirmed, 239 F.3d 104 (1st Cir. 2001). (1st Cir. 2001).

A federal district judge rejected and permanently banned Rhode Island's prohibition, stating that the legislation is "vague and does not give physicians with adequate direction to discern what the Legislature has rendered illegal." In addition, the court ruled, that the law's language specified, and impermissibly restricted, the most routinely used second-trimester abortion procedure, D&E. The court also struck down the ban because it lacked a health exception and an adequate life exception.

The Governor of Rhode Island pursued an appeal in the U.S. Court of Appeals for the First Circuit even after the decision in Carhart. The Governor said the order should not apply to post-viability abortions. The First Circuit rejected this argument and upheld the district court's verdict overturning the prohibition in its entirety.

Utah: Utah Women's Clinic v. Walker, No. 2:04CV00408 PGC (D. Utah June 10, 2004) (order granting preliminary injunction); Utah Women's Clinic v. Walker, No. 2:04CV00408 PGC (D. Utah May 31, 2007) (order lifting injunction) (order lifting injunction).

In June 2004, a federal district judge granted a preliminary injunction to suspend the implementation of Utah's legislation barring so-called "partial-birth abortions." The Utah bill endangers women because it lacks a health exemption and has broad phrasing that outlaws safe abortions early in pregnancy.

After Carhart II, the federal district court removed the injunction and dismissed the lawsuit. The court decided that the Utah legislation reflected the federal statute established by the Supreme Court and consequently sustained the prohibition as lawful.

Virginia: Richmond Medical Center for Women v. Gilmore, 11 F. Supp. 2d 795 (E.D. Va 1998) (preliminary injunction), stayed, 144 F.3d 326 (4th Cir. 1998), stay lifted, 183 F.3d 303 (4th Cir. 1998), 55 F. Supp. 2d 441 (E.D. Va. 1999) (permanent injunction), stayed, No. 98-1930 (4th Cir. Sept. 14, 1999), stay lifted, 219 F.3d 376 (4th Cir. 2000), affirmed, 224 F.3d 337 (4th Cir. 2000); Richmond Medical Center for Women v. Hicks, 301 F. Supp. 2d 499 (E.D. Va. 2004), affirmed, 409 F.3d 619 (4th Cir 2005), petition for rehearing denied, 422 F.3d 160 (4th Cir. 2005), cert. granted, judgment vacated, Herring v. Richmond Medical Center for Women, 127 S.Ct. 2094 (2007), remanded to 527 F.3d 128 (4th Cir. 2008), reversed en banc, 570 F.3d 165 (4th Cir. 2009). (4th Cir. 2009).

In Virginia's first effort to restrict safe abortions, a federal district judge imposed a permanent injunction to suspend the implementation of Virginia's "partial-birth abortion" ban. In permanently enjoining the act, the district court held that 1) the act created an undue burden because its plain language prohibited many common pre-viability D&E procedures, 2) the act was unconstitutional because it lacked a health exception and had an inadequate life exception, and 3) the act was void for vagueness. The U.S. Court of Appeals for the Fourth Circuit initially stayed the permanent injunction pending appeal. After the Supreme Court issued its ruling in Carhart, however, the Fourth Circuit lifted the stay and affirmed the district court's judgment invalidating the ban.

Despite the Fourth Circuit's decision, Virginia enacted a second law banning so-called "partial-birth infanticide." Although its wording is different, this second law suffers from the same flaws. Based on the Carhart decision, the district court struck the law because it contained no exception to protect women's health, contained only an inadequate exception to protect their lives, and its "plain language" would ban "pre-viability D&Es" and thus impose "an impermissible undue burden on the constitutional right to choose an abortion." The Fourth Circuit affirmed and denied a motion for a rehearing. The Supreme Court granted certiorari and vacated the judgment, remanding for further reconsideration in light of Carhart II. On remand, the Fourth Circuit affirmed that the Virginia ban was still unconstitutional under Carhart II because the act "lacks the intent and distinct overt act requirements that were central to the Supreme Court's decision."

Unlike the federal legislation, the Virginia measure criminalized all "intact D&Es," even if the practitioner had meant to execute another, legitimate abortion method. The measure consequently put an excessive barrier on a woman's right to get an abortion. The State appealed, and the Fourth Circuit overturned the panel ruling en banc. The court held that the facial challenge to the ban failed to "present a sufficiently frequent circumstance to render the Virginia act wholly unconstitutional." Moreover, the ban's scienter language provided sufficient notice of the prohibited conduct to doctors, and other safeguards in the ban prevent it from "creating a barrier to" or chilling a woman's right to a "standard D&E."

West Virginia: Daniel v. Underwood, 102 F. Supp. 2d 680 (S.D. W. Va. 2000).
(S.D. W. Va. 2000).

Following the decision in Carhart, a federal district court issued a permanent
injunction against the enforcement of West Virginia's ban. The court held the ban
unconstitutional because it: 1) "fails to provide an exception for the preservation of
the health of the woman" and 2) "prohibits D&E, in addition to D&X [dilation and
extraction] and therefore violates the 'undue burden' principle."

Wisconsin: Planned Parenthood of Wisconsin v. Doyle, 9 F. Supp. 2d 1033 (W.D.
Wis. 1998) (denying preliminary injunction), reversed, 162 F.3d 463 (7th Cir.
1998), remanded, 44 F. Supp 2d 975 (W.D. Wis. 1999) (denying permanent
injunction), vacated by Hope Clinic v. Ryan, 195 F.3d 857 (7th Cir. 1999), (en
banc) (remanding in favor of defendants), stay denied, 197 F.3d 876 (7th Cir.
1999), vacated and remanded, 530 U.S. 1271 (2000), 249 F.3d 603 (7th Cir. 2001).
(7th Cir. 2001).

A panel of the U.S Court of Appeals for the Seventh Circuit preliminarily enjoined
Wisconsin's "partial-birth abortion" ban after a federal district court refused to
issue emergency relief. On remand, however, the district court again refused to
impose an injunction but delayed its order pending an appeal to the Seventh
Circuit. The Seventh Circuit heard the case (together with the appeal of the order
enjoining Illinois's prohibition, see above). Initially, a thin majority of the court,
meeting en banc, maintained the Wisconsin legislation. The 5-4 decision was
issued over a vigorous dissent written by the chief justice. Finally, after the
Supreme Court issued the decision in Carhart, the Seventh Circuit held the
Wisconsin ban was unconstitutional and permanently enjoined its enforcement.

February 2012

(1) AL, AK, AZ, AR, FL, GA, ID, IL, IN, IA, KS, KY, LA, MI, MS, MO, MT, NE,
NJ, NM, ND, OH, OK, RI, SC, SD, TN, UT, VA, WV, WI
(2) AL, AK, AZ, AR, FL, ID, IL, IA, KY, LA, MI, MO, MT, NE, NJ, OH, RI, VA,
VW, WI. Before Carhart II, in Montana and Ohio, the states adopted further

restrictions, which were challenged and upheld on narrow grounds. After Carhart II, bans mirroring the federal ban were also upheld in Missouri and Utah, and a ban in VA also survived a court challenge. See, a summary of court decisions by state, below.
(3) IN, MS, MT, NM, OK, SC, SD, TN

(4) AZ, AR, KS, LA, MI, ND, OH, UT, VA

Chapter 2

Indiana becomes the first US state post-Roe to prohibit most abortions
Republican governor Eric Holcomb passes a measure into law that drastically
limits access to abortions with very few exceptions

Indiana's state legislature has become the first in the US to enact new laws limiting
access to abortions after the federal highest court overruled Roe v Wade.

The measure proceeded to the state's Republican governor, Eric Holcomb, who
signed it into law on Friday night.

Indiana was among the early Republican-run state legislatures to discuss stricter
abortion regulations following the supreme court verdict in June that erased
constitutional safeguards. It is the first state to approve a ban via both houses.

The Indiana senate passed the near-total prohibition 28-19, hours after house
members supported it 62-38. It offers limited exceptions, including in situations of
rape and incest, and to safeguard the life and physical health of the mother. The
exclusions for rape and incest are restricted to 10 weeks post-fertilization, meaning
victims may not seek an abortion in Indiana beyond that. Victims would not be
needed to sign a notarized document attesting to an incident.

The Kansas victory proves that Democrats can fight for abortion rights and win |
Moira Donegan
Outside the parliamentary chamber, abortion rights protestors regularly yelled over
lawmakers' statements, brandishing posters like "Roe roe roe your vote" and
"Build this wall" between religion and state. Some house Democrats donned
jackets over pink "Bans Off Our Bodies" T-shirts.

Indiana legislators heard evidence over the last two weeks in which citizens on both sides of the issue seldom, if ever, backed the measure. Abortion-rights proponents felt the law went too far, while anti-abortion groups said it did not go far enough.

In arguing against the measure, Rep Ann Vermilion blasted her fellow Republicans for labeling women who procured abortions "murderers".

"I believe that the Lord's promise is for grace and kindness," she remarked. "He would not be rushing to condemn these women."

The House rejected, primarily on party lines, a Democratic plan to include a non-binding question on the statewide November election ballot: "Shall abortion stay legal in Indiana?"

The Indiana House speaker, Todd Huston, indicated that if citizens were displeased, they could vote for new representatives.

Kansas voters had resoundingly rejected a bill that would have enabled the state's Republican-controlled legislature to limit abortion in the first test of voters' sentiments about the subject after Roe was reversed.

Indiana's proposed prohibition also came after the political tempest over a 10-year-old rape victim who flew to the state from neighboring Ohio to stop her pregnancy. The case grabbed notice when an Indianapolis doctor stated the infant moved to Indiana because of Ohio's "fetal heartbeat" prohibition.

Democratic Rep Maureen Bauer spoke emotionally before Friday's vote about individuals in her South Bend district who oppose the measure - the spouses standing behind their wives, the dads backing their children – as well as the women "who are asking that we be treated as equal".

Bauer's statements were followed by boisterous chants from demonstrators in the corridor and modest applause from fellow Democrats.

"You may not have expected that these ladies would turn up," Bauer added. "Maybe you assumed we wouldn't be paying attention."

West Virginia lawmakers on 29 July gave up the opportunity to be the first state with a unified prohibition when its lower house declined to agree with senate changes that eliminated criminal consequences for doctors who performed illegal abortions. Delegates instead requested a conference committee to review the specifics of the proposals.

Chapter 3

Indiana Governor Signs First Post-Roe Abortion Ban, With Limited Exceptions
The measure passed despite splitting Republicans. Some of them believed the bill
was too restrictive; others objected to limited exclusions for rape and incest.

Indiana legislators approved and the governor signed a near-total ban on abortion
on Friday, overcoming dissension among Republicans and complaints from
Democrats to become the first state to write out and implement extensive new
regulations on the practice since Roe v. Wade was knocked down in June.

The law's passing came only three days after voters in Kansas, another
conservative Midwestern state, decisively rejected an amendment that would have
deleted abortion rights provisions from their State Constitution, a decision
considered nationwide as an indication of concern with abortion prohibitions. And
it occurred despite several Indiana Republicans opposing the proposal for going
too far, and others voting no because of the exclusions.

Tracking the States Where Abortion Is Now Banned The New York Times is
monitoring the status of abortion restrictions in each state after the Supreme Court
decided to overturn Roe v. Wade.
The loss of Roe was the result of decades of struggle by conservatives, opening the
way for states to severely limit abortion or outlaw it outright. Some states prepared
in advance with abortion laws that were triggered by the demise of Roe.
Lawmakers in other conservative states suggested they might seek tougher limits.

But, at least in the first weeks following that decision, Republicans have moved
slowly and have failed to speak with a single voice on what comes next.
Lawmakers in South Carolina and West Virginia have debated but taken no final

action on proposed restrictions. Officials in Iowa, Florida, Nebraska, and other conservative states have so far not taken legislative action. And particularly in the past several weeks, some Republican lawmakers have recalibrated their message on the topic.

"West Virginia tried it, and they stepped back from the cliff. Kansas tried it, and the people resoundingly rejected it," State Representative Justin Moed, a Democrat from Indianapolis, said on the House floor before voting against the plan. "Why is that? Because up until now it has simply been a hypothesis. It was simple for folks to declare they were pro-life. It was simple to see things so stark and white. But today, that theory has become reality, and the ramifications of the ideas are more real."

The Indiana bill — which bans abortion from conception except in some cases of rape, incest, fatal fetal abnormality, or when the pregnant woman faces the risk of death or certain severe health risks — was signed into law within minutes of its final passage late Friday night by Gov. Eric Holcomb, a Republican who had encouraged legislators to consider new abortion limits during a special session that he called.

"These steps followed several days of hearings packed with sobering and personal testimony from residents and political leaders on this emotive and complicated topic," Mr. Holcomb said in a statement. "Ultimately, their voices molded and impacted the ultimate wording of the law and its carefully negotiated exclusions to handle some of the unimaginable scenarios a woman or unborn child would face."

Beyond those few exclusions, the new legislation will abolish legal abortion in Indiana next month. The treatment is now authorized at up to 22 weeks of pregnancy. Some Republicans have suggested that they anticipate the measure to be challenged in court.

"If this isn't a government issue – safeguarding life — I don't know what is," said Representative John Young, a Republican who backed the proposal. He added: "I

realize the exclusions are not enough for some and too much for others, but it's a
nice balance."

A First: The governor of Indiana signed a near-total ban on abortion, becoming the
first state to draw up and approve sweeping new limits on the procedure in the
post-Roe era.
A Resounding Decision: Kansas voters overwhelmingly rejected an amendment
that would have removed the right to abortion from the State Constitution, a major
win for the abortion rights movement in a deep-red state.
Shifting Gears: Republican candidates are softening their stands against abortion,
recognizing that strict bans are unpopular and that the issue could play a big role in
the midterm elections.

Fetal Personhood: The Department of Revenue in Georgia, where abortions are
illegal after six weeks, declared that fetuses may be claimed as dependents,
broadening the state's already an expansive definition of a fetus as a person.
The law's adoption came after two weeks of emotional testimony and contentious
deliberations in the Statehouse. Even while Republicans enjoy strong majorities in
both houses, the bill's fate did not always look assured. When a Senate committee
considered an initial version of the bill last week, no one showed up to testify in
support of it: The American Civil Liberties Union of Indiana called it a "cruel,
dangerous bill," and Indiana Right to Life described it as "weak and troubling,"
and a parade of residents with differing views on abortion all urged lawmakers to
reject it.

The discussion was intensified by the example of a 10-year-old Ohio girl who had
flown to Indiana for an abortion after she was raped. The abortion practitioner in
that instance, Dr. Caitlin Bernard, became a target of those on the right.

Abortion rights demonstrators were a frequent presence at the Statehouse
throughout the session, occasionally yelling "Let us vote!" or "Church and state!"
so loudly from the corridor that it may be impossible to hear politicians. Several
Democrats referenced the vote in Kansas, in which 59 percent of voters voted to

protect abortion rights, as an example of the political danger Republicans were taking. Democrats urged putting the subject to a nonbinding statewide vote in Indiana, which Republicans refused.

"Judging by the results I saw in Kansas the other day," said Representative Phil GiaQuinta, a Democrat who opposed the Indiana measure, "independents, Democrats, and Republicans by their votes proved what is most important to them, and me, and that is our liberties and liberty."

Todd Huston, the Republican speaker of the Indiana House, said he was happy with the final text of the measure. But questioned about the demonstrations in Indianapolis and the vote in Kansas, he conceded that many disagreed.

"We've talked about the fact that voters have an opportunity to vote, and if they're displeased, they'll have that opportunity both in November and in future years," Mr. Huston said.

Democrats warned of the consequences of passing the measure and noted the state's status as the first to do so in a post-Roe America. Business leaders sounded their concern before its passage: The chamber of commerce in Indianapolis urged the Legislature this week not to pass the bill, saying it could threaten public health and the state's business interests.

On Saturday, the pharmaceutical company Eli Lilly, a major employer in Indiana, said in a statement that because of the law, "We will be forced to plan for more employment growth outside our home state."

State Senator Eddie D. Melton, a Democrat who represents sections of northwest Indiana, testified against the measure on the Senate floor on Friday, calling it a hasty procedure and a power grab.

He reminded Republicans of the landslide victory in Kansas this week in favor of abortion rights, a warning to Indiana legislators that the party might suffer a backlash from voters.

"If this passes, the only referendum that's left is in November," he remarked.

Jennifer Drobac, a law professor at Indiana University Bloomington, said she was worried about the speed with which the measure in her state was approved and the relatively limited window for the public to discuss its ramifications.

"Law enacted in haste is frequently terrible law," she remarked. "This emphasizes the reality that these individuals are not anticipating how difficult this law would be. This is going to affect thousands of individuals who become pregnant in Indiana alone."

Divisions within the Republican Party were regularly on show throughout the session. Representative Ann Vermilion defined herself as a staunch Republican. But said she feared the measure went too far, too fast.

"The U.S. Supreme Court decided to relocate the abortion rights to the state level, which has peeled an onion on the nuances of abortion, displaying layers and layers of such a tough issue that I, too, wasn't prepared for," Ms. Vermilion stated before voting against the measure.

Other Republicans echoed the complaints voiced during public testimony by anti-abortion residents, advocacy groups, and religious leaders. They questioned how lawmakers who portrayed themselves to voters as staunch abortion opponents were now forgoing an opportunity to pass a ban without exceptions for rape and incest. Some abortion opponents have argued that rape and incest, while traumatic, do not justify ending the life of a fetus that had no control over its conception.

"This bill justifies the wicked, those murdering babies, and punishes the righteous, the preborn human being," said Representative John Jacob, a Republican who also voted against the bill. He added: "Republicans campaigned that they are pro-life. Pro-life means for life. That is not simply some lives. That means all lives."

Similar battles have played out in West Virginia, where the House of Delegates approved a measure that would outlaw almost all abortions. But debate broke out when the Senate narrowly chose to eliminate criminal sanctions for medical practitioners who perform abortion illegally, citing worries that it might aggravate the state's current scarcity of health care personnel. The measure is delayed.

Delegate Danielle Walker, a West Virginia Democrat, said she felt the abortion vote in Kansas was a wake-up call for the more moderate fraction of Republican lawmakers.

"I believe they're seeing that people are turning out to the polls because the people don't want this, the people don't want it," Ms. Walker added.

Elizabeth Nash, the state policy analyst at the Guttmacher Institute, which supports abortion rights, said that Indiana offered a glimpse of the dynamic that could deepen in other legislatures in the coming weeks: the difficulty in pleasing their conservative base in the face of other public opposition to abortion restrictions.

"In Indiana, the lawmakers are currently between a rock and a hard place," she added. "They're between their base," which is demanding an abortion ban with no exception, "and members of the public who are saying, 'we support abortion access.' You can see how the politicians, who are weighing people's rights, are also looking at the next election."